Cool Careers in Science

Protect the Environment

Improve Public Health

Work Outdoors

Learn Skills for Success

Environmental
SCIENTISTS

3-D PRINTING SPECIALISTS

BIG DATA SPECIALISTS

ENVIRONMENTAL SCIENTISTS

GENETIC ENGINEERS

VISUAL EFFECTS ARTISTS

ALTERNATIVE REALITY DEVELOPERS

ARTIFICIAL INTELLIGENCE SCIENTISTS

COMPUTER GAME & APP DEVELOPERS

DRIVERLESS VEHICLE DEVELOPERS

DRONE PILOTS

ENTERTAINMENT ENGINEERS

FORENSIC SCIENTISTS

PROFESSIONAL HACKERS

RENEWABLE ENERGY WORKERS

ROBOTICS DEVELOPERS

Cool Careers in Science

Environmental
SCIENTISTS

ANDREW MORKES

MASON CREST
MIAMI

Mason Crest
PO Box 221876
Hollywood, FL 33022
(866) MCP-BOOK (toll-free)

Printed in the United States of America

First printing

9 8 7 6 5 4 3 2 1

HARDBACK ISBN: 978-1-4222-4657-3
SERIES ISBN: 978-1-4222-4654-2
E-BOOK ISBN: 978-1-4222-7159-9

Cataloging-in-Publication Data on file with the Library of Congress

Developed and Produced by National Highlights, Inc.
Interior and cover design: Jana Rade, impact studios
Interior layout: Annalisa Gumbrecht, Studio Gumbrecht
Production: Print Matters Productions, Inc.

QR CODES AND LINKS TO THIRD-PARTY CONTENT

Table of Contents

KEY ICONS TO LOOK FOR:

WORDS TO UNDERSTAND: These words with their easy-to-understand definitions will increase the reader's understanding of the text while building vocabulary skills.

SIDEBARS: This boxed material within the main text allows readers to build knowledge, gain insights, explore possibilities, and broaden their perspectives by weaving together additional information to provide realistic and holistic perspectives.

EDUCATIONAL VIDEOS: Readers can view videos by scanning our QR codes, providing them with additional educational content to supplement the text. Examples include news coverage, moments in history, speeches, iconic sports moments, and much more!

TEXT-DEPENDENT QUESTIONS: These questions send the reader back to the text for more careful attention to the evidence presented there.

RESEARCH PROJECTS: Readers are pointed toward areas of further inquiry connected to each chapter. Suggestions are provided for projects that encourage deeper research and analysis.

CAREERS IN SCIENCE OFFER GOOD PAY, THE OPPORTUNITY TO HELP PEOPLE, AND OTHER REWARDS

Where would we be without science? Well, we'd be without computers, smartphones, robots, and other cutting-edge technologies. Crimes would take longer to solve without modern forensic analysis techniques. We'd be stuck relying on environmentally unfriendly fossil fuels instead of using renewable energy. And life would be less fun, because we wouldn't have drones, awe-inspiring and physics-defying roller coasters, or the computer and video games that we play for hours.

Job markets are sometimes strong and sometimes weak, but a career in science (which, for the purposes of this series, includes the related fields of technology and engineering) is almost a sure path to a comfortable living. The following paragraphs provide more information on why a career in science is a great choice.

Good pay. People in science careers earn some of the highest salaries in the working world. The mean annual salary for those in life, physical, and social science careers in the United States is $79,360, according to the US Department of Labor (DOL). This is much higher than the mean earnings ($56,310) for all occupations. Those in engineering occupations earn $90,300, and computer and mathematics professionals earn $96,770. Science professionals who become managers or who launch their own businesses can earn anywhere from $150,000 to $300,000 or more.

Strong employment prospects. There are shortages of science workers in the United States, Canada, and throughout the rest of the world. The DOL predicts that employment of computer and information technology professionals in the United States will grow by 13 percent during the next decade, which is much faster than the average for all careers. Career opportunities for those in life, physical, and social science occupations will grow by 8 percent (as fast as the average), although many specialties will experience growth that is faster than the average. The outlook is also good for engineering professionals. Employment is expected to grow by 6 percent during the next decade. The strongest opportunities will be found in the rebuilding of infrastructure, oil and gas extraction, renewable energy, and robotics.

By 2030, the DOL predicts that there will be nearly one million new jobs in science, technology, engineering, and mathematics fields.

Rewarding work environment and many career options. A career in science is fulfilling, because you get to use both your creative and practical sides to develop new technologies (or improve existing ones), solve problems, and make the world a better place. In the case of environmental science, you get to collect and analyze information to protect our natural world and humans. Many careers in environmental science involve fieldwork to collect data and otherwise observe environmental conditions, but you'll also work in laboratories, research facilities, and even manufacturing plants. Some science professionals launch their own businesses, which can be both fun and very rewarding. Others choose to become teachers or write books and blog posts about environmental science topics.

Job opportunities are available throughout the United States and the world. Science professionals play such an important role in our modern world that there are job openings almost anywhere, although many positions are found in large, metropolitan areas.

IS A CAREER IN SCIENCE RIGHT FOR ME?

Test your interest. How many of these statements do you agree with?

___ My favorite classes are biology and environmental science.

___ I also enjoy chemistry and mathematics classes.

___ I like to conduct research and gather data.

___ I like to solve problems.

___ I enjoy doing science experiments.

___ I am curious about how things work.

___ I am creative and have a good imagination.

___ I enjoy being outdoors.

___ I care about protecting the environment and want to make the world a better place.

If many of the statements above describe you, then you should consider a career in environmental science. But you don't need to select an occupation right now. Check out this book on a career as an environmental scientist, and other books in the series, to learn more about occupational paths in the sciences and related fields. Good luck with your career exploration!

WORDS TO UNDERSTAND

environmental policy: a course of action a government establishes to manage how businesses, other organizations, and people use and interact with the natural world.

fracking: a drilling technique used to extract oil or natural gas from deep underground; studies show that fracking can cause air pollution, groundwater contamination, health problems, and surface water pollution.

interdisciplinary: drawing from two or more different fields of knowledge.

professional association: an organization that is founded by a group of people who have the same career (e.g., engineers or scientists), or who work in the same industry specialty (e.g., waste management or health care).

remediation: the process of cleaning up or using other strategies to remove or contain a toxic spill or hazardous materials.

Chapter 1

ENVIRONMENTAL SCIENCE AND CAREERS

WHAT IS ENVIRONMENTAL SCIENCE?

Environmental science is an **interdisciplinary** field in which scientists, engineers, technicians, and other science professionals conduct research on plants, animals, and entire ecosystems and study environmental problems that have been caused by both the actions of humans and natural processes. People who work in environmental science have educational backgrounds and training in the physical and biological sciences (biology, chemistry, ecology, zoology, oceanography, atmospheric science, soil science, physics, and earth sciences such as geology and hydrology), engineering (especially chemical, environmental, hazardous waste management, and wastewater), and the social sciences (human geography, environmental planning, and environmental economics, and other fields).

Environmental scientists try to make the world a better place by conducting research and identifying and solving environmental problems. Their work seeks to reduce the damage caused by global warming and climate change, ozone depletion, destruction of forests and other natural areas, soil erosion, oil spills, and toxic chemicals released during industrial processes. They study the effects that energy exploration and extraction techniques such as **fracking** have on the environment, try to protect endangered and threatened animal and plant species (and entire ecosystems), and help companies ensure that they are in compliance with environmental regulations. That's just the tip of the iceberg when it comes to describing the work of environmental scientists.

Learn more about environmental science.

DID YOU KNOW?

Nearly 36 percent of people surveyed by the World Economic Forum said that human-caused damage to the environment presents a "clear and present" danger to the stability of the world.

Global warming and melting of the polar ice caps are two major problems environmental scientists study.

CAREER PATHS IN ENVIRONMENTAL SCIENCE

The following paragraphs provide more information about career paths in environmental science.

Agricultural scientists conduct research on the biological and chemical processes that allow crops and livestock to grow, as well as develop strategies to improve the quality, quantity, and safety of agricultural products. They specialize in fields such as soil, plant, animal, and food science.

Atmospheric scientists study the layer of gases, called the *atmosphere*, that surrounds the earth, as well as conduct research on the weather and climate to determine how they affect humans, plants and animals, and the overall environment. Specialists include *meteorologists,* who study the lower parts of the atmosphere (primarily the troposphere) and its effects on our weather; *climatologists,* who study historical weather patterns to interpret long-term weather patterns or shifts in climate to better understand ongoing global climate change; and *climate scientists,* who work on the theoretical foundations and the modeling of climate change in order to help **environmental policymakers** base decisions about strategies to reduce negative climate change, design buildings that are more resilient to adverse weather events, better plan efficient land use and agricultural production, and meet other goals.

Biologists study various aspects of animal and plant life, such as their origins, anatomy, relationships, development, and functions. They can specialize in a variety of fields. For example, *wildlife biologists* study specific ecosystems or animal populations, such as a particular at-risk species, or focus on the conservation and management of wildlife populations. *Microbiologists* analyze tiny living things that can only be seen with a microscope, such as fungi, bacteria, viruses, and algae.

Chemists study substances at the atomic and molecular levels to determine their makeup and to see how they interact with nonliving and living things. *Environmental chemists* are specialized chemists who study the effects that various chemicals have on the air, soil, and water and their cumulative effects on plants, animals, and ecosystems, as well as humans. They specialize in areas such as waste management and the **remediation** of contaminated soils, air, and water. *Biochemists* study chemical processes and chemical transformations in living organisms and entire ecosystems.

Climate change analysts study scientific data and conduct research about the effects of climate change on the environment. They make climate-related recommendations for potential legislation, awareness campaigns, or fundraising; write grant proposals; and engage in environmental outreach activities.

Conservation scientists protect and manage forests, parks, rivers, rangelands, and other natural resources. Specialized career paths in conservation science include *conservation land manager, forester, range manager, soil conservationist,* and *water conservationist.*

Ecologists study the relationships among organisms and habitats of many different sizes, from the study of bacteria, fish, and crabs in a tidal pool near the Pacific Ocean to the thousands of species of plants, animals, and other organisms that live in Yellowstone National Park. *Industrial ecologists* are specialized ecologists who work in industrial settings to identify environmental

Learn about the top 10 major global environmental issues in the world.

impacts caused by products, systems, or projects and provide solutions to reduce those impacts.

Environmental health and safety specialists identify and investigate how environmental factors and issues (e.g., pollution, soil and water contamination caused by manufacturing, deforestation) affect human health, and educate the public about environmentally based health risks.

Environmental restoration planners visit sites that have been polluted by chemicals, radiation, and other harmful substances to determine the cost, work hours, and steps that will be required to clean up the area. They work closely with environmental engineers, geologists, biologists, and other professionals to develop habitat management or restoration plans.

Environmental toxicologists investigate the effects of toxic materials and chemicals on humans, plants, animals, air, water, soil, and the overall environment. One example of their work might involve being hired to collect and analyze soil and water samples at the site of a former gas station that will be converted to residential use, in order to assess the risk of chemical contamination to the air, water, and soil. If harmful contaminants are identified, the toxicologist determines what needs to be done to clean up the site.

Geologists study the earth's physical structure and the processes that create that structure. They collect information about rocks, air, water, and glaciers. *Environmental geologists* use their geological expertise to help clean up chemical spills and leaks that are located below and above ground and try to prevent future ones from occurring.

Geophysicists use their knowledge of physics, earth science, seismology (the study of earthquakes and related phenomena), and similar fields to study the surface and interior of the earth. *Environmental geophysicists* are specialized

An oceanographer studies "Wisdom," the oldest known living Laysan albatross (which is at least sixty years old) at Midway Atoll National Wildlife Refuge.

geophysicists who identify, map, or predict the presence and potential movement of groundwater and surface water in order to help locate safe sites for underground waste disposal. They also use their expertise to identify chemicals and other contaminants in the top 100 meters (or so) of the earth's surface.

Hydrologists conduct research on the distribution and use of groundwater and surface water, especially its movement in relation to the land. They study how changes to the environment influence the quality and quantity of water.

Oceanographers study the world's oceans, including the physical and chemical properties of the water, marine organisms, ocean circulation, plate tectonics and the geology of the seafloor, and other topics.

Zoologists conduct research to improve our understanding of particular types of animals, such as birds or amphibians, as well as study how environmental and climatological issues affect the health and welfare of animals. Some examples of specialized zoologists include *cetologists,* who study marine mammals, such as dolphins, porpoises, and whales; *herpetologists,* who study reptiles and amphibians, such as snakes, turtles, alligators, and frogs; and *ornithologists* who study birds, such as hawks, herons, swifts, penguins, and cranes.

Some environmental scientists work closely with *environmental engineers,* who find solutions to a variety of environmental problems and issues such as climate change, pollution, drought, deforestation, flood protection, and waste management. Others help to develop renewable energy resources. For example, an environmental engineer in the wind industry will study how a potential wind farm project may negatively affect wildlife and plants, create noise issues, and potentially interfere with radar and telecommunications systems and provide strategies to address these issues. They may also work with wind farm developers to ensure that they are in compliance with environmental regulations and policies.

Laboratory technicians and technologists provide support services to environmental scientists by setting up and organizing laboratory equipment and supplies, conducting basic tests, and inputting and analyzing data.

Environmental science and protection technicians collect air, soil, water, and other types of samples for laboratory analysis and make observations about environmental conditions that helps scientists protect the environment and solve environmental problems. They set up and maintain pollution-monitoring

A science technician collects water samples from the Chicago River for testing.

equipment, perform tests on samples on-site and in the laboratory, and write reports and prepare visual presentations that summarize their findings.

DID YOU KNOW?

Sixty percent of Americans surveyed by the Pew Research Center in 2019 had a "mostly positive" view of environmental research scientists. Twenty-nine percent had "neither a positive nor negative" view, and 14 percent had a "mostly negative" view of these professionals.

EMPLOYERS OF ENVIRONMENTAL SCIENTISTS

There are opportunities for environmental scientists in the public, private, and nonprofit sectors.

PUBLIC SECTOR

The US Department of Labor estimates that 40 percent of environmental scientists work for federal, state, and local government agencies. At the federal level, scientists, engineers, technicians, and other environmental science professionals are employed by the Environmental Protection Agency, National Oceanic and Atmospheric Administration, National Park Service, National Renewable Energy Laboratory, US Department of Agriculture, US Fish and Wildlife Service, US Forest Service, US Geological Survey, US Department of Energy, and other agencies. They also work in non-environment–focused agencies, such as the US Department of State (in its Office of Global Change, which is responsible for implementing and managing US international policy on climate change). Other employment opportunities are found in state and local departments of natural resources, environmental protection agencies, and other employers. Some environmental scientists work in the US military and in the armed forces of other nations as environmental health and safety officers and specialists, meteorologists, oceanographers, physical scientists, and water and sewage treatment plant operators.

US RENEWABLE ENERGY USE BY SOURCE

Renewable energy makes up nearly 13 percent of all energy used in the United States. Here are the most popular forms of renewable energy:

Bioenergy (biomass waste, biofuels, wood): 39.1 percent of all renewable energy

Wind: 25.9 percent

Hydroelectric: 22.4 percent

Solar: 10.7 percent

Geothermal: 1.8 percent

Source: US Energy Information Administration

PRIVATE SECTOR

Environmental professionals are employed by companies of all sizes and work in research, land reclamation, wastewater treatment, engineering services, and many other areas. They also help manufacturers to develop more environmentally friendly products, improve production processes to reduce pollution emissions or improve efficiencies to save energy, and ensure corporate compliance with environmental regulations. The renewable energy and electric vehicle sectors are also major employers of environmental professionals.

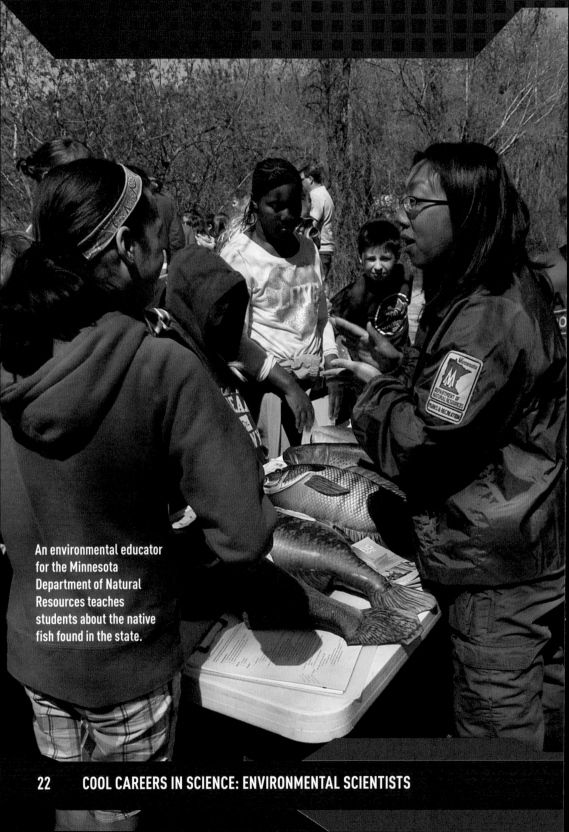

An environmental educator for the Minnesota Department of Natural Resources teaches students about the native fish found in the state.

NONPROFIT ORGANIZATIONS

A nonprofit organization (which is also known as a *nonprofit*) is a group that uses any money it generates to advance its stated goals. It is not a corporation or other for-profit business. A wide range of nonprofits employ environmental scientists. Environmental research organizations (such as Earthwatch Institute, Cary Institute of Ecosystem Studies, and the Global Energy Network Institute) conduct independent scientific research, and some offer opportunities for training and fieldwork. There are also environmental advocacy organizations (such as the Natural Resources Defense Council, Greenpeace, Environmental Defense Fund, and The Nature Conservancy) that seek to shed light on pressing environmental issues and encourage policymakers, businesses, other organizations, and the public to better protect the environment. Some organizations, such as The Nature Conservancy, also purchase and manage land that contains rare ecosystems or other valuable natural resources. Environmental professionals also work at nonprofit colleges and universities as researchers, professors, and administrators, and as executives and staff at **professional associations**.

SELF-EMPLOYMENT

Experienced scientists and other environmental professionals can start their own consulting businesses and provide services and expertise to government agencies and businesses. Some work as writers or independent researchers.

WORK ENVIRONMENT

Work conditions for environmental scientists vary greatly based on their employer, job title, and other factors. Some scientists spend their entire workdays in laboratories, while others work in offices or on the floor of a

Some environmental scientists spend a considerable amount of time conducting research in wintry and other adverse conditions.

bustling and noisy manufacturing plant. Others spend the majority of their time outdoors conducting field research, collecting samples, and performing other duties. Environmental science professionals who work outdoors encounter a variety of weather conditions—from humid, sunny days, to rainy or wintry ones. They must be in excellent physical shape, because they often walk long distances to reach research sites or track wildlife, which can sometimes be dangerous. (Examples include wolves, bears, sharks, and poisonous insects and reptiles.) Some scientists live in rustic campsites for days or weeks at a time as they conduct research. Most people who enter this type of environmental

Some environmental scientists spend nearly all of their time conducting research in laboratories.

scientist position love the outdoors and consider this aspect of their career a professional perk rather than a drawback.

Many environmental scientists work a standard 40-hour, Monday-through-Friday week, while others work at night and on weekends.

Most environmental scientists enjoy their work because it is intellectually engaging and constantly changing and because their work helps to protect the environment. In fact, 74 percent of environmental scientists who were surveyed by PayScale.com reported that they were "highly satisfied" with their careers.

ENVIRONMENTAL SCIENCE CAREER PATH

Skilled and hardworking scientists can be promoted to positions in management, start a consulting firm, or work in other high-level positions. Here is a typical career ladder for environmental science professionals:

Consulting firm owner or environmental science professor
Science executive
Science manager
Senior environmental scientist
Entry-level environmental scientist
Environmental science and protection technician

ADVANCEMENT

With experience and a proven record of quality work, environmental scientists can advance by receiving pay raises and being assigned supervisory duties. Some companies have managerial training programs that prepare scientists for supervisory positions. Managers can advance to executive-level positions such as vice president of research, laboratory manager, or even president or chief executive of their organization. Environmental scientists with an entrepreneurial mindset may choose to launch their own consulting firms and provide services and expertise to government agencies, businesses, and other organizations. Consultants have the potential to earn considerably higher salaries than salaried scientists do, but being a business owner involves a higher level of risk and time commitment because they must constantly seek out new clients, manage staff, and handle challenges such as malfunctioning computers and clients who do not pay their bills. Some scientists decide to work as college professors or even as high school science teachers. Others choose to write books, journal articles, and blog posts about environmental science–related topics.

TEXT-DEPENDENT QUESTIONS:

1. Can you name three types of physical or biological sciences?
2. What are some environmental science specialties?
3. What is a hydrologist?

RESEARCH PROJECT:

Conduct research to identify three emerging environmental problems that will affect the world in the next ten years. What types of careers will emerge in relation to these problems? Write a 500-word report that provides more information about your research, and present your findings to your science class or environmental club.

Chapter 2

TERMS OF THE TRADE

Air pollution: A mixture of harmful human-made and natural substances in the air we breathe.

Atmosphere: The layers of air that surrounds the earth.

Atmospheric science: The study of the layers of gases, called the *atmosphere*, that surround Earth.

Biodiversity: A term that describes the variety of plants, animals, and microorganisms, and their interaction within habitats and ecosystems.

Bioenergy: Energy that is produced from non-fossilized plant materials, such as wood and wood waste.

Bioremediation: The act of using microorganisms (usually naturally occurring), such as bacteria, fungi, or yeast, to break down hazardous substances and pollutants.

Brownfields: Unused or underused industrial and commercial land that may be contaminated by toxic chemicals and other hazardous waste.

Carbon dioxide: A colorless, odorless gas that is naturally present in Earth's atmosphere. It is an important part of plant growth on Earth, but if too much is released because of the burning of fossil fuels—such as coal and oil—it can cause global warming and damage the environment.

Carbon footprint: The amount of greenhouse gas (e.g., carbon dioxide, methane, and ozone) emissions created by a person, product, organization, building, or event; greenhouse gases warm the earth's atmosphere and cause climate change.

Climate change: Changes to the environment caused by both natural and human-created processes. One major source of climate change is the release of excess amounts of carbon dioxide, which is caused by the burning of fossil fuels such as coal and oil.

Climate: The pattern of weather in a particular area or region over a set period, typically studied over a thirty-year span. Climate is affected by the amount of precipitation, levels of humidity, wind speed the topography (the natural and artificial features of an area), and other factors.

Composting: The practice of adding organic material to soil to help plants grow; compost has three basic ingredients: water, browns (branches, dead leaves, and twigs), and greens (vegetable waste, fruit scraps, grass clippings, and coffee grounds).

Computer modeling: Using a software program to predict the results of a process or series of events.

Conservation: Protecting animals, plants, and other resources through planned action, such as reseeding prairies, breeding endangered species, or preserving rare areas of land.

Data analysis: The process of studying and making conclusions about pieces of information.

Deforestation: Cutting or burning down a forest so that the land can be converted to bare ground and used for agriculture.

Drought: A prolonged period of little or no rain that creates or worsens a shortage of water.

Ecofriendly: A product or action that does not hurt the environment.

Ecosystem: A biological community of living things and the environment they live in.

Effluent: Liquid wastes, such as sewage and discarded industrial fluids, that are discharged from a factory or other source into a natural body of water.

Emissions: Gases or particles that are released into the air. They contribute to poor air quality and global warming.

Energy: Thermal (heat), light (radiant), kinetic (motion), electrical, chemical, nuclear, or gravitational energy that is harnessed to perform the functions of life.

Deforestation.

Fertilizers: Natural or chemical substances that are added to the soil to help make plants grow better.

Fossil fuels: Nonrenewable energy sources such as crude oil, natural gas, and coal that were formed millions of years ago by natural processes inside the earth.

Fracking: A drilling technique used to extract oil or natural gas from deep underground. Studies show that fracking can cause air pollution, groundwater contamination, health problems, and surface water pollution.

Genetically modified crops (GMCs): Those that have been genetically altered by scientists so that they have higher nutritional value; improved yields; increased resistance to frost, drought, or insect pests; longer shelf life; and other benefits. Debate continues about the safety of GMCs and genetically modified animals.

Genetics: A branch of science that studies how specific traits are passed from parent to offspring.

Geographic Information Systems (GIS): Computer technology that collects and analyzes data about the physical features of the earth's surface.

Geology: The study of the earth's physical structures and the processes that create that structure.

Geosciences: The study of the earth's structure and the processes that shape it.

Global warming: The heating of the earth that is caused by the release of heat-trapping gases (called *greenhouse gases*) as a result of the burning of fossil fuels and other activities. Greenhouse gases allow sunlight to enter the earth's atmosphere, but trap heat that typically radiates into space. The use of renewable energy plays a major role in reducing greenhouse gas emissions.

Greenhouse gases: Gases such as methane, nitrous oxide, and carbon dioxide that trap heat radiating from the earth's surface and cause warming in the lower atmosphere.

Groundwater: Water that is located beneath the ground surface in the soil, sand, or rock.

Habitat: The place where plants, animals, and other organisms traditionally live.

Hazardous waste: Waste that can damage human health and the environment and that must be handled and disposed of carefully. Examples include weed killers, bleach, oil-based paints, and car batteries.

Hydrology: The study of the movement, distribution, and quality of water in the earth and its relationship with the environment.

Invasive species: A living organism such as plant, animal, insect, fish—or even an organism's seeds or eggs—that does not naturally occur in a specific ecosystem and that can cause harm.

Meteorology: The study of the lower parts of the atmosphere (primarily the troposphere) and its effects on our weather. It is a specialized field of atmospheric science.

Nonrenewable energy: Types of energy that cannot be replaced after use; these include coal, petroleum, and natural gas.

Nutrients: Substances that plants and other living things need in order to grow and that they cannot entirely make on their own.

Ocean acidification: A negative change in the chemical makeup of the ocean.

Outdoor air pollution: A mixture of harmful human-made and natural substances in the outdoor air. Outdoor air pollution consists of fine particles produced by the burning of fossil fuels, ozone, noxious (harmful or poisonous) gases (such as sulfur dioxide, nitrogen oxides, carbon monoxide, and chemical vapors), tobacco smoke, and other components.

Ozone layer: A region of the stratosphere (a layer of the earth's atmosphere) that absorbs the most harmful components of the sun's ultraviolet radiation. These components can cause skin cancer and cataracts as well as damage to crops and marine life. Also known as **ozone shield**.

Ozone: A naturally occurring gas (in small, trace amounts) in the upper atmosphere (the stratosphere) of the Earth. Ozone is created by chemical reactions between air pollutants from vehicle exhaust, gasoline vapors, and other emissions.

Pesticide: Any substance or mixture of substances that is used to prevent, destroy, repel, or reduce the presence of a pest (such as insects, weeds, and mold). In large amounts, pesticides can be harmful to both humans and the environment.

Plant genetics: Studying and working with the genes of plants to make them healthier or make them produce more fruits and vegetables.

Pollution: The contamination of the air, water, or soil with chemicals or other foreign substances that are detrimental (harmful) to human, animal, or plant health, or to entire ecosystems.

Recycle: To break down waste items (such as packaging, plastic, tin cans) into their raw materials so that they can be used to make new items.

Reforestation: Planting trees in areas that previously contained forests.

Remediation: The process of cleaning up or using other strategies to remove or contain a toxic spill or hazardous materials.

Renewable energy: Sources of energy that never run out and that cause less damage to the environment than fossil fuels (coal, petroleum, natural gas). The main types of renewable energy are solar, wind, hydropower, geothermal, and

View of wind turbines on Prince Edward Island in Canada.

bioenergy. Renewable energy sources typically have no or low environmental impact. Also called **alternative energy** or **clean energy**.

Researcher: A specially trained person who seeks to find answers to difficult questions.

Scientific method: A procedural method that scientists follow in order to answer questions about the world. The scientific method consists of observation, hypothesis, experimentation, and interpretation.

Scientific paper: A special type of written work that is published in a journal, is reviewed for accuracy by other professionals in the field, follows a standardized style of writing and data presentation, is citable, and includes citations.

Seismology: The study of earthquakes and related phenomena.

Smog: Air pollution that consists of smoke (and other pollution) and fog. Smog, which frequently occurs in large urban and industrial areas, can damage plant life and cause breathing problems and eye irritations in humans.

Soil erosion: A naturally occurring process in which topsoil is worn away by the natural physical forces of wind and water.

Soil nutrients: Those that provide energy to plants for growth. The three main nutrients are nitrogen, phosphorus, and potassium. Other important nutrients include calcium, sulfur, and magnesium.

Soil pollution: The contamination of soil by chemicals or other foreign substances that are harmful to human, animal, or plant health, or to entire ecosystems. Examples include pesticides, asbestos, lead, petroleum products, radon, and other chemical and waste products.

Solid wastes: A variety of municipal wastes that include discarded food, newspapers, bottles, cans, old cars, construction debris, and disused furniture.

Sustainability: An emphasis on implementing building practices that save energy or reduce energy output, that use building materials from renewable resources such as wood and stone that can also be recycled or reused, and that incorporate other environmentally friendly practices.

Sustainable agriculture: Farming practices that seek to protect and preserve the environment for future use by farmers. Sustainable agriculture aims to promote a healthy environment while still achieving economic profitability (making money) and social and economic equity (fairness).

Thermal pollution: An increase in temperature in the air, water, and soil, sufficient to result in ecological change.

Topsoil: The uppermost layer of soil that typically is the richest in organic matter and microorganisms that help crops grow.

Toxin: Something that is dangerous, or even fatal, to an organism.

Toxicology: The study of the adverse (negative) effects of chemicals on living organisms.

Waste management: The way in which waste (including feces, urine, and garbage) is collected, cleaned, and disposed of.

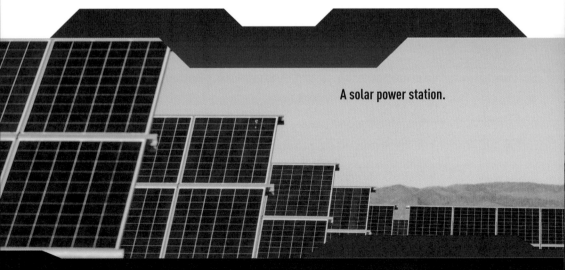

A solar power station.

Waste: Any discarded materials.

Wastewater: Used water from a home, community, farm, commercial building, or manufacturing plant that contains dissolved or suspended matter. Wastewater can contain human waste, soaps and chemicals, food scraps, oils, and other substances.

Water habitats: The wet places where plants, animals, and other organisms traditionally live.

Water pollution: The contamination of water with chemicals or other foreign substances that are harmful to human, animal, or plant health, or to entire ecosystems. Examples include sewage and food processing waste; fertilizers and pesticides from agricultural runoff; mercury, lead, and other heavy metals; chemical wastes from industrial discharges; and chemical contamination from hazardous waste sites.

Zoology: The study of animals.

WORDS TO UNDERSTAND

capstone: in academia, a final class that seeks to summarize all that a student has learned in a program.

certification: a professional credential that one earns by passing a test and meeting other requirements, and which improves the chances of getting a job and earning higher pay.

cooperative education opportunities: a structured method of learning that involves both classroom-based education and practical work experience; students who complete a cooperative education experience often receive academic credit.

discussion boards: websites at which people who have the same interests can meet and share conversations, photos, and videos about that interest and related topics.

recruiter: a person or business that searches for job candidates for a company or other organization.

Chapter 3

PREPARING FOR THE FIELD AND MAKING A LIVING

EDUCATIONAL PATHS

A minimum of a bachelor's degree is needed for entry-level jobs as environmental scientists, but some employers require a minimum of a master's degree in the field or their specialty (e.g., environmental chemistry, environmental engineering, earth science). A few aspiring environmental scientists first received training to work as chemists or atmospheric scientists, or in other science-related positions in the military. After leaving the military, they earned a certificate or degree in environmental science or a related field, or they took classes in those and other areas to build their skills. The following sections provide more information on educational preparation.

HIGH SCHOOL CLASSES

In high school, be sure to take as many science classes as possible to build your skills and knowledge. Recommended courses include environmental science, biology, chemistry, and physics. Environmental scientists should be excellent communicators (both orally and in writing), so you should take English, writing, and speech classes. Many scientists in the United States collaborate with science professionals in other countries. For that reason, it's a good idea to take a foreign language to improve your ability to communicate with people who do not speak English fluently. If you become proficient (skilled) in a foreign language, you will have the option to work and teach in the country (or countries) where that language is used. Other recommended classes include

- Computer science (because scientists use computers to store and analyze data)
- Data analytics (to learn how to study data)
- Mathematics (to learn how to work with numbers)
- Philosophy (to develop your critical thinking skills)
- Social studies (to obtain a better understanding about past and current events)

TYPES OF EDUCATION CREDENTIALS

A **certificate** shows that a person has completed specialized education, passed a test, and met other requirements to qualify for work in a career or industry. College certificate programs typically last six months to a year.

A student earns an **associate's degree** after they complete two years of post–high school education at a community or technical college.

Students study water samples collected from a nearby stream.

A student earns a **bachelor's degree** in one of two ways:

- By earning an associate's degree and completing two additional years of education at a four-year college or university
- By graduating from high school and completing four years of education at a four-year college or university

A **master's degree** is a graduate-level credential that is awarded to a student after they first complete a four-year bachelor's degree and then two additional years of education.

A student earns a **doctoral degree** after first earning a bachelor's and master's degree. To earn a doctorate (also known as a **PhD**), students must conduct original research, prepare a dissertation (a type of long report), and defend their dissertation before a committee of professors.

A graduate student conducts research on Eastern Cottonwood saplings. (Jason Richards, Oak Ridge National Laboratory)

COLLEGES AND UNIVERSITIES

Many people train for this field by earning a bachelor's or graduate degree in environmental science and also earning a certificate in a specialty (e.g., chemistry or atmospheric science) to augment their skills. Others first earn a bachelor's degree in environmental science and then earn master's degrees and PhDs in a specialty.

Many people who work in environmental science have degrees in the physical and biological sciences (e.g., biology, chemistry, ecology, zoology, oceanography, atmospheric science, soil science, physics, and earth sciences such as geology and hydrology), engineering (especially chemical, environmental, hazardous waste management, and wastewater), or the social sciences (human geography, environmental planning, environmental economics, and other fields).

Typical classes in a bachelor's-level environmental science program include:

- Applied ecology
- Biostatistics
- Earth system science
- Environmental data analysis
- Environmental science and studies capstone **Capstone**
- Environmental soil science
- Freshwater and wastewater science
- Geographic information systems
- Human impacts on the environment
- Introduction to environmental health
- Research methods

Professors and students discuss the bachelor of science in environmental sciences program at Northern Arizona University.

THE BEST UNIVERSITIES FOR ENVIRONMENT/ECOLOGY IN THE UNITED STATES

US News & World Report recently ranked the top programs in environment/ecology in the United States. Here are the top ten:

1. Stanford University (Stanford, CA)
2. Harvard University (Cambridge, MA)
3. University of California-Berkeley
4. University of Minnesota-Twin Cities (Minneapolis/St. Paul)
5. University of Washington (Seattle)
6. Yale University (New Haven, CT)
7. University of California-Santa Barbara
8. Princeton University (Princeton, NJ)
9. Duke University (Durham, NC)
10. University of Colorado-Boulder

Visit www.usnews.com/education/best-global-universities/united-states/environment-ecology for the complete list.

You'll need a master's degree in business management, project management, or science management to be eligible for managerial and executive positions at many employers. If you decide to teach environmental science at a college or university, you'll need at least a master's degree but preferably a doctoral degree. If you'd rather teach environmental science at the high school level, you'll only need a bachelor's degree.

Most colleges require students to participate in an internship or other experiential learning opportunity as part of their training. An internship is a paid or unpaid learning opportunity in which you work at a business, government agency

Interns in the Sustainable Agriculture Systems Laboratory at the Agricultural Research Service conduct experiments.

(such as the National Renewable Energy Laboratory, Environmental Protection Agency, or National Park Service), or nonprofit organization (such as the Student Conservation Association) to get experience. It can last anywhere from a few weeks to a year. Duties for environmental science interns vary by employer, but you might be tasked with collecting data in forests, swamps, or other natural settings or conducting experiments and other research in laboratories. Your professors and/or your college's career services office can help you find internships. Another strategy is to contact employers directly about potential internship opportunities. The federal government offers many jobs and internships for those who are interested in environmental science. Visit the US Office of Personnel Management's website, www.usajobs.gov, to learn more about opportunities with federal agencies. Many young people cite internships as one of the key tools to both learn about career options and land a job, so be sure to participate in at least one internship or other experiential learning opportunity while you are in school.

APPRENTICESHIPS

Most people associate apprenticeships with training opportunities in the skilled trades, but a growing number of employers are offering apprenticeships in environmental science as an alternate or ancillary educational option. Environmental science apprenticeships are more common in European countries such as the United Kingdom and Germany, but they are slowly growing in popularity in the United States. For example, the US Environmental Protection Agency (EPA) offers the Environmental Research Apprenticeship Program for College and University Students, which allows participants to interact with scientists, develop effective scientific research and technical skills, and build their knowledge base. Apprenticeship programs typically last from one to three years. Apprentices receive a salary while they learn, and their earnings increase as they obtain experience.

MILITARY

Let's be honest, the military is not the first provider that comes to mind when one thinks of training to become an environmental scientist. But the world's militaries place a high value on the work of environmental scientists to assess the viability of building or expanding military bases, identify and clean up pollution on military bases, remove pollutants from water supplies, and accomplish many other mission-critical tasks.

If you're interested in a career in environmental science, the branches of the US military (Air Force, Army, Coast Guard, Marines, and Navy) offer a variety of training opportunities. Some will give you direct experience with environmental science, while others will provide a good knowledge base that you can build on once you leave the military. The following military careers are good options for those interested in environmental science:

- Environmental health and safety officer
- Environmental health and safety specialist
- Meteorologist
- Oceanographer
- Physical scientist
- Water and sewage treatment plant operator

Visit Today'sMilitary.com to learn more about these and other careers. Some militaries in other countries also provide science training. If you do not live in the US, contact your country's armed forces for more information on training opportunities.

Serving in the military is a good way to receive free training (and a salary and room and board while you're doing so), but it is not for everyone. The military will be a good fit if you do not mind following orders, possibly being assigned to a desolate base in a country that is thousands of miles from home (remember, not everyone gets a posting in a tropical place like Hawaii or a cultural mecca such as Germany or Japan), and are willing to make a service commitment of two to four years. If you decide to join the military, talk with a representative from the recruiting office to learn about science-related careers and other information that will help you to make an informed decision. Be sure to obtain a promise in writing that you will be assigned to your target job after you enlist. After all, you don't want to end up being forced to serve in the infantry when you had your heart set on working as a physical scientist.

Attending a job fair is a good way to learn about prospective employers.

GETTING A JOB

You've had it pretty good for many years. Your parents pay for your education, put a roof over your head and feed you, and buy whatever essentials you need. But there will come a time in your life when you need to get a job and pay for these things yourself. You may already have a part-time job that's providing some real-world experience and money to pay for things that your parents don't buy for you. Congrats! You've taken the first step to becoming an adult. Although you don't have to get a full-time job and become an adult yet, it's never too early to learn how the job search process works (especially if you've never had a job).

What are a cover letter and résumé? What is a job interview? How does one get a job? These are common questions that young people may ask themselves when thinking about the job search for the first time.

A cover letter is a one-page letter that details one's interest in a job and their qualifications. A résumé is a formal summary of one's educational and work experience that is submitted to a potential employer. Cover letters and résumés can be sent in hard-copy form or digitally. Some people consider one's LinkedIn profile to be a form of résumé, and some people have websites that serve as online versions of their cover letter and résumé. A job interview is a formal meeting in which you discuss your qualifications for a job with a potential employer. It can be conducted in-person, via telephone, or via an online communication platform. Some employers require applicants to participate in just one interview before offering them a job, while others ask applicants to participate in multiple interviews. You can find additional information about cover letters, résumés, and job interviews by talking to career counselors at your school, parents, family members and friends who have jobs, and your teachers, as well as checking out books and websites.

You may already be familiar with job search strategies but, if not, here are some popular methods. Use as many of these strategies as you can during your job search to improve your chances of landing a job. You can also use these strategies to obtain internships and other experiential learning opportunities.

USE YOUR NETWORK

There are many stereotypes about networking. For example, some people think you can't network until you're in the workforce. Others believe that you can only network in person, while still others believe the entire process of networking is fake and insincere.

These perceptions are all incorrect. Before we address these myths, let's define networking, which is simply the process of developing relationships with people to obtain information and learn about internships, **cooperative**

education opportunities (often known as *co-ops*), and job opportunities. As to the aforementioned myths regarding networking, you can begin networking while you're in high school, and for sure no later than college. You can certainly network at in-person events, but many people do it via email, instant messaging, and online communication platforms, as well as through social networking sites such as LinkedIn. And, finally, networking is not fake or insincere. Both sides should benefit from networking relationships, and some people who network even become friends because of their shared professional interests and the rapport that develops by helping each other meet personal and professional goals.

It's estimated that 70 to 85 percent of jobs are found through networking, so it's important that you begin building your network as soon as possible. Did you know that you already have a personal network that consists of your friends, classmates, and family? You've used that network to get answers to questions about homework, sports tryouts, clubs, and other activities. Many people land their first part-time jobs in schools due to leads offered by members of their personal networks. If you're looking for a job or an internship, spread the word to your personal network. For example, your mom's friend may work as an environmental scientist at a local laboratory, or your friend's brother may currently work as an intern at the Environmental Protection Agency and might be able to connect you with the internship director.

As you get older, you'll also become part of a professional network. This network is made up of your teachers, internship directors, bosses, coaches, current and former coworkers, classmates, and people you meet online, including through LinkedIn and other social networking sites. Members of your professional network can be especially helpful, because they have worked closely with (or managed) you and know your strengths and weaknesses.

Your high school or college science teacher can become a key member of your network.

CHECK OUT JOB BOARDS

Internet job boards list internship and job openings. They are offered by professional associations, businesses, publishers of professional journals, and other organizations. While you're not ready for a full-time job or most likely even an internship, reviewing job listings provides you with valuable information about typical job duties for a profession and the education and skills that are in demand. Here are some environmental job boards and career pages:

- https://environmentalcareer.com

- www.renewableenergyjobs.com

- www.energy.gov/eere/education/find-jobs

- www.awma.org/careers
- www.acs.org/content/acs/en/careers.html
- www.esacareercenter.org
- https://jobbank.wef.org
- www.careerplacement.org
- www.science.org/careers
- https://eco.ca/new-practitioners/employment-support/job-board

And here are some general job sites that offer environmental science job listings:

- www.indeed.com
- www.linkedin.com
- www.jobbank.gc.ca (Canadian government job board)
- www.gov.uk/find-a-job (United Kingdom government job board)

JOIN AND USE THE RESOURCES OF PROFESSIONAL ASSOCIATIONS

These organizations will be great resources for you as a student and a professional. Many provide membership, publications, education and career information, networking opportunities, **discussion boards**, continuing education (CE) classes and webinars, and other resources that will help you advance in your chosen profession. The Ecological Society of America (www.esa.org) is a good example of a quality environmental association. It offers membership for college students and professionals; online access to its journals, such as *Ecology, Ecological Applications,* and *Frontiers in Ecology and the Environment;* CE opportunities, **certification**, and a directory of certified professional ecologists (which you can use as a resource to identify potential contacts for networking). Here are some other professional associations for environmental science professionals:

- American Academy of Environmental Engineers and Scientists: www.aaees.org
- American Water Resources Association: www.awra.org
- American Geosciences Institute: www.americangeosciences.org
- American Institute of Biological Sciences: www.aibs.org

OTHER WAYS TO FIND A JOB

Here are a few additional ways to land a job:

- Attend job fairs that are sponsored by your college or employers.
- Hire a **recruiter** to help you to identify job leads.
- Visit the websites of potential employers to learn about and apply for jobs.
- Develop a strong presence on social media in your occupational field in order to get noticed by potential employers.

HOW MUCH CAN I EARN?

Environmental scientists and specialists earn average salaries of $80,090, according to the US Department of Labor. That is much higher than the average salary ($56,310) for all careers. Earnings range from $42,960 to $129,450 or more.

Salaries for environmental scientists vary, based on their educational background and level of experience, whether they work full- or part-time, and other factors. For example, a scientist who has ten years of experience will likely earn a much higher salary than a new hire straight from college. Earnings also vary by employer. For example, the average salary for environmental scientists who work at federal agencies is $105,060, while those who work at state agencies ($70,530) and local agencies ($73,580) tend to earn less.

Earnings for environmental scientists and specialists also vary by job title. The following are salary ranges for workers in different occupations.

- Atmospheric and space scientists: $52,350–$153,150[+]
- Biochemists and biophysicists: $52,640–$169,860[+]
- Chemical engineers: $68,430–$168,960[+]
- Chemists: $44,970–$139,650[+]
- Conservation scientists: $39,230–$100,350[+]
- Environmental engineers: $55,450–$144,670[+]
- Geoscientists (except hydrologists and geographers): $51,890–$201,150[+]
- Hydrologists: $52,900–$130,030[+]
- Microbiologists: $45,690–$156,360[+]
- Soil and plant scientists: $39,650–$117,450[+]

TEXT-DEPENDENT QUESTIONS:

1. What high school classes should you take to prepare for a career in environmental science?
2. What types of environmental science–related career options are available in the military?
3. What is the salary range for environmental scientists?

RESEARCH PROJECT:

Learn more about the typical classes and other requirements to earn a degree in three of the following majors: environmental science, environmental engineering, environmental chemistry, hazardous materials management, and environmental science and sustainability. Visit the websites of colleges in your area that offer these programs, and try to talk with professors about the programs. Design a poster for each major that presents typical classes in each program, comments from the professors and/or the schools' websites, and other information that will be useful to those seeking to learn more about these majors. Perhaps you could incorporate photos from the programs. Present this information to your science class or club or during your school's career day.

WORDS TO UNDERSTAND

conference: an event at which members of an organization, and sometimes the public, meet to discuss and learn more about a topic, such as global warming.

earth Day: an annual event that is observed each April 22 to educate people about the environment and inspire them to protect it; the first Earth Day was in 1970.

mentor: an experienced professional who provides advice to a student or inexperienced worker (mentee) regarding personal and career development.

scholarship: money that is awarded to a student to pay for college and other types of education; it does not have to be paid back.

Chapter 4

KEY SKILLS AND METHODS OF EXPLORATION

SKILL BUILDING LEADS TO SUCCESS

It takes a variety of technical and soft skills to be successful in environmental science. Technical skills consist of one's computer expertise and knowledge, as well as the ability to use equipment in laboratories and in the field. These skills vary by profession and industry. *Soft skills* are personal abilities that people need to develop to be successful in a job—communication, work ethic, teamwork, decision-making, positivity, time management, flexibility, problem-solving, critical thinking, conflict resolution, and other abilities and traits.

Regarding technical skills, environmental scientists need to know how to use a wide variety of equipment—from microscopes to gas chromatographs in the laboratory to air samplers or collectors, soil core samplers, water samplers and analyzers, radiation detectors, and other environmental monitoring and testing equipment and geographic information systems technology in the field.

They also must know how to use computer modeling software, which predicts the results of a process or series of events; map creation software; pollution modeling software; emissions tracking software; data collection and analytics software; other types of scientific software; and word processing, presentation, and graphics or photo imaging software. Technical knowledge varies by specialty, so it's a good idea to talk with environmental scientists about required technical skills, to get a more detailed idea of what is required for your target profession.

While technical skills and knowledge are important, many employers place equal importance on soft skills, because those play a significant role in one's success on the job and their ability to work well with others. Here are some important soft skills.

ANALYTICAL, RESEARCH, AND PROBLEM-SOLVING SKILLS

Most environmental issues (e.g., global climate change, coral reef bleaching, and soil degradation) are complex and evolving problems. As a result, you will need to methodically gather and study environmental data to make scientific conclusions. This type of research takes patience, diligence, and a micro-focus on the key details that will help you to gain insights into the problem and devise a solution (or solutions) to the problem, while factoring in how its implementation will affect nearby ecosystems and human communities.

COMMUNICATION SKILLS

Environmental scientists must be masters of both the written and spoken word in order to communicate with colleagues, but also to translate complex terminology and concepts into easy-to-understand language. Writing skills (including

Strong communication and interpersonal skills are important for success as an environmental scientist.

expert knowledge of proper grammar and spelling) are important, because scientists must write clear and concise reports and journal articles that synthesize their research and recommendations. Presentation skills are also important, because environmental scientists speak about their work to the media, make presentations at environmental **conferences**, and communicate with others about their work via online videoconferencing technology. Finally, strong listening skills are important, because scientific research involves collaboration with other scientists. If you fail to keep your mind open to the work and insights of others, you may end up duplicating research or pursuing research paths that other scientists have already exhausted.

INTERPERSONAL SKILLS

Although scientists often spend a good amount of time conducting research on their own, many large research projects involve collaboration with other scientists, environmental engineers, science technicians, and other professionals in laboratories, other research facilities, and in the field (often under demanding or remote conditions). As a result, you should be comfortable working with people of different ages and genders, as well as those from different cultures and backgrounds. To be successful as a member of a team, you must be patient, friendly, a good listener, willing to compromise, and accepting of other people's work habits and opinions.

Successful environmental scientists have a detail-oriented personality and don't mind getting dirty—or wet—as they do their jobs.

OTHER SKILLS

Here are some other important traits for environmental scientists:

- Curiosity
- Attention to detail
- The ability to work under deadlines
- Passion for science and research
- Self-motivation and self-discipline
- Good time management
- Leadership (if you work in management or own a consulting business)
- Business skills (if you decide to launch a business)
- A willingness to continue to learn

EXPLORING ENVIRONMENTAL SCIENCE AS A STUDENT

There are many ways to learn more about environmental science and careers in the field. Start out by reading books such as *Environmental Science: A Global Concern,* by William and Mary Ann Cunningham, and visiting websites. Here are some other popular methods of exploration.

TAKE A CLASS

You'll certainly get your fill of science-related classes in high school, but did you know that you can learn about environmental science via online and in-person courses that are offered by online learning platforms such as Udacity, Coursera, edX, and Udemy; private organizations; professional associations; and other providers? For example, Udemy offers courses called Introduction to Environmental Chemistry, Understanding Environmental Pollution, and Environmental Ecosystem and Natural Resources. Some courses are even free or available for under $20.

Another option is to take classes at a community college while you are still in high school. That will allow you to build your knowledge of topics that you haven't yet studied in school and to learn what it's like to attend college. (It's a lot different from high school.) Some colleges even allow high school students to earn college credit for completed coursework. That is a great way to get a head start on your college degree and save on your education expenses, because the cost of taking community college classes is lower than the cost of courses at a four-year college.

DID YOU KNOW?

Fifty-nine percent of teens surveyed by the National Environmental Education Foundation in 2017 felt that the environment was in bad shape but that it could be saved. Forty-five percent believed that the health of the environment would get worse in the future. Fifty-nine percent of teens worried about the state of the environment.

JOIN THE TECHNOLOGY STUDENT ASSOCIATION (TSA)

The TSA (https://tsaweb.org) is a national nonprofit organization for middle and high school students who are interested in science, technology, engineering, and mathematics. Becoming a member of TSA will help you to develop your leadership skills, receive certification from CompTIA (an IT trade association), and compete for money for college. Another cool aspect of this organization is that it offers sixty competitions at its annual conference—including those in IT fundamentals, coding, software development, cybersecurity, and technology problem-solving. These competitions are a good way to test your abilities, meet new people, build your network, and have some fun. Ask your computer science teacher or school counselor whether your school has a TSA chapter; if not, ask them to start one.

START A CLUB

You high school may already have an environmental or nature club that you can join to learn more about the environment. If not, then work with your science teacher and school counselor to start one. Here are a few activities that are often offered by such clubs:

- Learn about activities to improve the environment, such as recycling, water conservation, and composting.
- Listen to presentations about careers by environmental scientists.
- Plant trees on **Earth Day** and at other times of the year.
- Help install solar panels and rain barrels at your school.
- Listen to presentations by admissions officers about educational opportunities in environmental science at area colleges.
- Take field trips to laboratories, nature centers and museums, wind farms, solar farms, and other environmental sites.
- Learn about environmental issues such as pollution, global climate change, and deforestation.

CONDUCT RESEARCH

Some people think that you must be a scientist—or at least a college student—to conduct research, but that's not true. You may not realize it, but you are

Members of a high school Environmental Awareness Club have some fun after conducting environmental research.

conducting research when your science teacher asks you to conduct an experiment, collect and test water samples from a local pond, or even write a research paper about global climate change. There are also formal training programs for middle and high school students that will help you to learn how to conduct research and gain new insights about science topics. For example, the American Geophysical Union (AGU), a professional association for earth and space scientists, offers the Bright Students Training as Research Scientists (Bright STaRS) program in which middle and high school students who are participating in after-school and summer research experiences in the earth and space sciences present their research to their classmates and others of the same age, as well as to scientists and the scientific community at the AGU's fall meeting. Meeting attendees can also visit the Academic Showcase, which offers information on forty institutions that offer college geoscience programs; and they can attend a shadowing program to observe scientific sessions. Learn more at www.agu.org/Learn-and-Develop/Learn/Student-Competitions/Bright-Stars. Other research options are available from the Smithsonian Environmental Research Center (https://serc.si.edu/high school), which offers field studies for high school students on its 2,650-acre research campus, as well as research-based programs for the classroom.

ATTEND A SUMMER CAMP

Colleges and universities, high schools, community groups, park districts, museums, and other organizations and groups provide summer camps and programs that will help you to learn more about environmental science, explore potential career paths, learn how to conduct research, and make some new friends. Ask your science teacher or a school counselor to direct you to camps in your area.

Summer camps focusing on environmental science are available in several countries. Here are some examples of well-known camps in the United States:

The National Student Leadership Conference offers thirty summer programs that help high school students learn more about a particular field. Its nine-day Environmental Science & Sustainability Program is held several times a summer in New Haven, Connecticut. Participants study soil and water samples under the supervision of marine biologists and ecologists in a laboratory, learn about the world's most pressing environmental issues, attend talks by guest speakers (such as the head of the Environmental Protection Agency), work on a conservation project that emphasizes natural resource management, and participate in other activities. Other programs are available in marine biology and engineering, and they are located in cities around the United States. Learn more at www.nslcleaders.org.

Michigan Technological University (MTU) offers several opportunities for high school students who are interested in exploring STEM fields, including its Summer Youth Program, in which students in grades 6 through 11 can take week-long exploratory sessions. Participants can commute or live on campus. Recent sessions included Aquatic Ecology, Environmental Invaders, Introduction to Renewable Energy, Wildlife Ecology, and Wild World of Chemistry. Those who are interested in exploring engineering (including environmental, chemical, and geological engineering) in a college setting can participate in MTU's Engineering Scholars Program and Women in Engineering Program. Learn more at www.mtu.edu/syp.

The US Department of Agriculture offers AgDiscovery, a two- to four-week residential summer outreach program for teens who are interested in exploring careers in plant and animal science, forestry, wildlife management, and other fields. Students obtain experience in these fields through hands-on labs, workshops, and field trips. Learn more at www.aphis.usda.gov/aphis/ourfocus/civilrights/agdiscovery/ct_agdiscovery_program.

A variety of overnight and day STEM- and agriculture-focused camps are offered by 4-H. If you live in the United States, the best way to learn about opportunities in your area is to visit https://4-h.org/parents/ways-to-participate/4-h-camps and search for the 4-H office in your county. Camps in some states are also listed at this website. Camps run by 4-H are also available in Canada and other countries.

Finding More Camps

Many other colleges, universities, organizations, and businesses offer summer STEM camps. Contact schools and organizations in your area to learn more.

CAMP INFO

- Most camps are offered during the summer, but some are scheduled during holiday breaks and at other times during the year.
- Some camps charge a fee to cover program costs and room and board (lodging and food). This fee can be very low (under $50) or high (hundreds to thousands of dollars), depending on the program's length, its sponsor, and other factors. Scholarships that cover all or some of the cost of attendance may be available. Some camps are even free.
- Residential (you'll live on-site in a college dormitory or other comfortable building) or day (you'll go home after each session) options are available.
- Camps can last anywhere from a few days to a month or more.
- Camps are becoming a popular option for students seeking to explore careers and potential college majors, so you'll need to register as soon as possible to guarantee yourself a spot.
- Some postsecondary schools that offer summer programs offer college credit for completing a program. Check with your target programs to see whether this is an option.

Learn more about the Maine Envirothon.

Students compete in the National Science Bowl

PARTICIPATE IN A COMPETITION

Environmental associations and organizations, colleges and universities, high schools, and other organizations sponsor contests that allow you to test your abilities and knowledge against others who are interested in environmental science and other STEM fields. Check out the following competitions:

The National Science Bowl is a nationwide academic competition for teams of middle and high school students that tests their knowledge in all areas of science and mathematics. It's sponsored by the US Department of Energy's Office of Science. The National Science Bowl is one of the largest science competitions in the United States. Learn more at https://science.osti.gov/wdts/nsb.

The Stockholm Junior Water Prize International Competition is open to students in grades 9 through 12 who have conducted a water science research project that aimed to enhance the quality of life through improvement of water quality, water and wastewater treatment, or water resources management at the local, regional, national, or global level. Applicants must have reached the age of fifteen by August 1 of the competition year. The contest consists of four levels: regional, state, national, and international. Applicants must use scientifically accepted methodologies for experimentation, monitoring, and reporting of their findings. Learn more at www.wef.org/resources/for-the-public/SJWP.

High school-aged students in the US and Canada who would like to test their knowledge of environmental issues, ecosystems, and topography can enter the National Conservation Foundation Envirothon competition, which is held over six consecutive days each summer in a different US state or Canadian province each year. Teams demonstrate their knowledge of environmental science and natural resource management at five training/testing stations: Aquatic Ecology, Current Environmental Issue, Forestry, Soils/Land Use, and Wildlife. Winners receive scholarships, prizes, and accolades. Learn more at www.envirothon.org/the-competition.

The Junior Science and Humanities Symposium (JSHS) is a competition for high school students who conduct STEM-related research investigations. Students first compete in a JSHS Regional Symposium, and winners advance to the National JSHS. Competitions are available in environmental science (bioremediation, ecosystems management, environmental engineering, land resource management, pollution, toxicity, impact upon ecosystems), chemistry (physical chemistry, materials science, alternative fuels, geochemistry), and other fields. Regional and national finalists receive undergraduate tuition scholarships and cash awards from the US Army, Navy, and Air Force. Learn more at www.jshs.org.

Other Competitions

Here are some additional contests to investigate

Marine Science Scholarship Competition for High School & Undergraduate Students: https://namepa.net/education/science-awards

National Ocean Sciences Bowl: www.nosb.org

Genius Olympiad: www.geniusolympiad.org

Young Champions of the Earth: https://web.unep.org/youngchampions

Students pose for a photo after competing in the Kodiak Envirothon.

SOURCES OF ADDITIONAL EXPLORATION

Contact the following organizations for more information on education and careers in environmental science:

American Academy of Environmental Engineers and Scientists
www.aaees.org

American Chemical Society-Division of Biological Chemistry
www.divbiolchem.org

American Geosciences Institute
www.americangeosciences.org

American Institute of Biological Sciences
www.aibs.org

American Institute of Hydrology
www.aihydrology.org

American Water Resources Association
www.awra.org

Association for Women Geoscientists
www.awg.org

Association for Women in Science
www.awis.org

Ecological Society of America
www.esa.org

Environmental Careers Organization of Canada
https://eco.ca

Institute of Hazardous Materials Management
www.ihmm.org

National Association of Environmental Professionals
www.naep.org

Society of Women Environmental Professionals
https://swepweb.com

VOLUNTEER

Volunteering is a great way to help a science organization or agency meet its goals, obtain hands-on experience, and make connections that may lead to a recommendation for college, or even a job. Volunteer opportunities of all types

Volunteers and scientists with the Environmental Protection Agency team up to collect water quality data and trash along a creek.

and time commitments are available from national, state, and local associations and government agencies, as well as environmental firms.

In the Natural Resources Conservation Service (NRCS) Earth Team Volunteers program, young people ages fourteen and older can work at one of 2,500 NRCS offices nationwide. As a NRCS volunteer, you work full-time or part-time in an office or remotely, or in the field with NRCS professionals as they help private landowners (farmers, ranchers, and foresters) put conservation practices in place that will improve the health of the soil, air, water, and wildlife. Learn more at www.nrcs.usda.gov/wps/portal/nrcs/main/national/people/volunteers.

The US Fish and Wildlife Service offers volunteer opportunities at more than 500 refuges and hatcheries throughout the United States. Volunteers of all ages and backgrounds are welcome. Duties vary, but past volunteers have restored habitat, rescued turtles, removed invasive plants, conducted plant and animal surveys, and helped at refuge events such as bird festivals. Learn more at www. fws.gov/volunteers.

The Nature Conservancy provides volunteer opportunities in the United States and throughout the world. Learn more at www.nature.org/en-us/get-involved/ how-to-help.

JOB SHADOW AN ENVIRONMENTAL SCIENTIST

Job shadowing is the process of following a worker around while they do their job, with the goals of learning more about a particular career and building one's network. It is a great way to learn more about a career, because you get to see the person who is actually doing the work. If you job shadow an environmental scientist, for example, you might get the chance to observe them as they take water samples from a nearby lake to determine why a massive fish die-off occurred, test the samples in a laboratory, and update managers or community members about their findings. Try to job shadow at least three environmental scientists, because they work in so many different specialties and job settings. Ask your science teacher or school counselor to help arrange information inter-views. You also could ask your parents whether they know any environmental scientists who might let you job shadow them. Local, state, and national profes-sional associations might also be able to direct you to potential candidates.

One related option is to observe an environmental science class at a local community college or four-year college. Many schools allow prospective students to sit in on freshman-level classes to get a feel for the school and to determine whether a specific major is a good fit for them. Perhaps your experience will make you realize that you'd rather be a professor than a practicing scientist.

CONDUCT AN INFORMATION INTERVIEW

If you are unable to arrange a job shadowing experience, you should try to participate in an information interview. In this type of interview, you ask environmental science professionals questions about their educational preparation, job duties, work environment, and other topics that will help you better understand the field. You can conduct your interview on the telephone, through videoconferencing software online, or via email.

Here are some questions to ask during the interview:

- Can you tell me about a day in your life on the job?
- Where do you work?
- Do you travel for your job? If so, to where and how often?
- What are the most satisfying/challenging/frustrating aspects of the job?
- What kind of technology and other tools do you use to do your work?
- What are the most important personal and professional qualities for environmental science professionals?
- Is your job stressful? If so, please explain why.
- How did you train for the field? What advice would you give to young people to be successful in college?
- What is the future employment outlook for environmental science professionals? How is the field changing?
- What can I do now to prepare for the field?
- What professional/trade associations do people in this field join?

FEDERAL ENVIRONMENTAL AGENCIES

Here are some of the major federal agencies that focus on environmental science, pollution control and monitoring, conservation, renewable energy, and related fields.

Environmental Protection Agency
www.epa.gov

Energy Information Administration
www.eia.gov/renewable

National Oceanic and Atmospheric Administration
www.noaa.gov

National Park Service
www.nps.gov

National Renewable Energy Laboratory
www.nrel.gov

US Department of Agriculture
www.usda.gov

US Fish and Wildlife Service
www.fws.gov

US Forest Service
www.fs.usda.gov

US Geological Survey
www.usgs.gov

US Department of Energy

Office of Energy Efficiency and Renewable Energy
www.energy.gov/eere/office-energy-efficiency-renewable-energy

OTHER WAYS TO LEARN MORE ABOUT ENVIRONMENTAL SCIENCE EDUCATION AND CAREERS

- Read books and watch videos about environmental science. Your school librarian and YouTube.com are good sources.
- Participate in online environmental science discussion boards.
- Attend environmental science conferences and other events.
- Participate in Earth Day activities in your community.

Young people plant a tree on Earth Day.

- Join the Boy Scouts or Girl Scouts, and earn merit badges in Environmental Science, Fish & Wildlife Management, Bird Study, Soil and Water Conservation, Chemistry, Engineering, Forestry, Insect Study, Oceanography, Plant Science, and other areas.
- Participate in an environment-related internship or part-time job.
- Visit the websites of college and university environmental science programs.
- Develop a relationship with a **mentor** to learn about education and careers in environmental science.
- Talk to your school counselor about career opportunities in environmental science.

TEXT-DEPENDENT QUESTIONS:

1. Why is it important for environmental scientists to be good communicators?
2. What types of resources are offered by the Technology Student Association?
3. What is the National Conservation Foundation Envirothon?

RESEARCH PROJECT:

Conduct information interviews and/or participate in job shadowing experiences with three to five different types of environmental scientists. Gather information about how they broke into the field, their job duties and work environment, what they like and dislike about their careers, how they trained for the field, and other topics. Write a 500-word report about your findings, and present it to your environmental club or science class.

WORDS TO UNDERSTAND

artificial intelligence: the simulation of human intelligence by machinery and computer systems.

data set: a collection of two or more data points.

environmental impact assessment: an evaluation to determine the potential positive and negative economic, human-health, and other impacts of a potential project, such as the construction of a wind farm.

remote sensing: the use of satellites or high-flying aircraft to collect information about areas of the earth.

retrofitting: the addition of new technology to existing systems in order to improve efficiency, reduce pollution, or meet other goals.

Chapter 5

THE FUTURE OF ENVIRONMENTAL SCIENCE AND CAREERS

THE BIG PICTURE

Our world faces a troubling array of environment problems, such as global climate change, pollution, deforestation, destruction of critical habitat for plants and animals, and the acidification of oceans. These issues are causing significant harm to humans, plants, animals, and the environment. If efforts aren't made to address and solve these problems, there will be long-term, irreversible damage to the earth, as well as significant financial costs for governments, businesses, other organizations, and everyday people. As a result, there is strong need for skilled environmental science professionals to conduct research on environmental problems, present solutions to address them, and develop practices that minimize waste, prevent pollution, reduce global warming, and conserve resources.

Job opportunities for environmental scientists and specialists are projected to grow by 8 percent from 2020 to 2030, according to the US Department of Labor

(DOL). That is about as fast as the average for all careers. Opportunities will be strongest for experienced scientists with master's and doctoral degrees who are skilled at using current and emerging technology to collect and study data. Job prospects for environmental scientists vary, based on one's industry employer. Stronger-than-average demand is expected in the following sectors:

- Support activities for mining: +39.3 percent
- Management, scientific, and technical consulting services: +22.4 percent
- Remediation and other waste management services: +18 percent
- Waste management and remediation services: +17.2 percent
- Professional, scientific, and technical services: +14.7 percent
- Waste treatment and disposal: +12.6 percent

Declining or slower-than-average job growth is expected in the following sectors:

- Fossil fuel electric power generation: -30.9 percent
- Electric power generation: -28.2 percent
- Natural gas distribution: -7.4 percent
- Federal agencies: -1.4 percent
- State agencies: -0.4 percent
- Oil and gas extraction: +0.2 percent
- Manufacturing: +3.9 percent

It's important to remember that you can still land a job in a sector with weak employment demand. If you really have your heart set on working as an environmental scientist in a particular sector (such as with the federal government), you will just need to work extra hard to land that dream job. Top-notch grades in college Singular, strong personal and professional networks, demonstrated enthusiasm when interacting with potential employers, and considerable internship and related experience will also help you to land a job.

Many people are attracted to careers in environmental science because they provide opportunities to work outdoors in scenic areas. Above, a hydrologist measures streamflow on Government Gulch Creek, a tributary to the Coeur d'Alene River in northern Idaho.

EMPLOYMENT GROWTH BY CAREER

The following sections provide more information on expected employment demand for select environmental careers through 2030 (according to the DOL).

AGRICULTURAL SCIENTISTS

Demand for agricultural scientists will increase by 9 percent (or as much as the average for all careers) due to the need to feed growing populations, meet increasing demand for water resources, address changes in climate and weather patterns, and satisfy additional demand for agriculture products, such as biofuels.

BIOCHEMISTS AND BIOPHYSICISTS

Employment for biochemists and biophysicists is expected to grow by 5 percent. That is slower than the average, but the DOL reports that there will be strong demand for those who work in the areas of clean energy, environmental protection, and efficient food production.

CONSERVATION SCIENTISTS

Job opportunities for conservation scientists will increase by 6 percent, or about as fast as the average for all occupations. Conservation scientists will be needed to conduct research on habitat destruction, restoration, and conservation; the prevention and suppression of wildfires; and the effects of global climate change on forests, grasslands, lakes and other waterways, and other natural areas. Conservation scientists with expertise in the use of Geographic Information System (GIS) technology, **remote sensing**, and other software tools will have the best job prospects.

ENVIRONMENTAL ENGINEERS

Although overall employment for environmental engineers will grow by only 4 percent (slower than the average), there will be steady demand for those environmental problem solvers, because there are so many pressing issues that need to be addressed, such as helping government agencies (especially at the state and local levels) improve water-use efficiency and help to identify and clean up contaminated sites. In the private sector, environmental engineers will be needed to advise companies (especially in the energy and utility industries) regarding wastewater treatment and disposal (such as from hydraulic fracking), compliance with federal or state environmental regulations (such as regulations regarding emissions from coal-fired power plants), **retrofitting** existing manufacturing facilities to make them more environmentally friendly, and other environmental issues. Job demand will be strongest in the motor vehicle manufacturing (+32.4 percent); remediation and other waste management services (+18 percent); management, scientific, and technical consulting services (+16.3 percent); and waste treatment and disposal (+12.6 percent) sectors. Employment at local government agencies is expected to increase by 8.3 percent.

GEOSCIENTISTS

Job opportunities for geoscientists (a career category that includes geochemists, geologists, oceanographers, geophysicists, and other science professionals) will increase by 7 percent due to the need for energy, environmental protection, and responsible land and resource management. Geoscientists are playing an increasing role in the renewable energy industry, and demand will be stronger in that sector than in other sectors.

HYDROLOGISTS

Concerns about global climate change; rising sea and lake levels in some areas, and drought in others; and damage to and the overuse of water resources due to mining, construction, and fracking will create steady demand for hydrologists. Employment will increase by 6 percent, but it's important to remember that this field is small and that there will be only a small number of job openings available. Despite the critical role that hydrologists play in developing comprehensive water management plans for government agencies, funding for hydrology positions (especially at the state and federal levels) will be tight.

WILDLIFE BIOLOGISTS AND ZOOLOGISTS

Job opportunities for wildlife biologists and zoologists are projected to grow by 5 percent (slower than the average for all careers). These professionals will be needed to study human and wildlife interactions as human populations increasingly negatively affect wildlife and their natural habitats; develop and implement conservation plans that protect animals, plants, and entire ecosystems; and find solutions to a variety of other environmental issues, such as invasive species, habitat loss, pollution, and climate change.

ENVIRONMENTAL SCIENCE AND PROTECTION TECHNICIANS

Demand for environmental science and protection technicians is projected to grow by 11 percent, faster than the average for all careers. Technicians play an

A team of wildlife biologists walk into the river to retrieve fish eggs for study.

important role in performing support tasks for environmental scientists and engineers who are conducting research on topics such as the effects of fracking on the environment, global warming, and deforestation and other types of habitat destruction. Businesses and government agencies will increasingly rely on technicians to help monitor environmental conditions and comply with regulations. When budgets are tight, many employers hire technicians as a cost-effective substitute for scientists in low-level positions. With advanced education, some technicians earn bachelor's and advanced degrees in order to qualify for higher-level science positions.

ENVIRONMENTAL SCIENCE COLLEGE TEACHERS

Employment for postsecondary environmental science teachers is projected to increase by 7 percent (as fast as the average for all careers). Despite the prediction for steady growth, it will be difficult to land a tenure-track position, because there is low turnover for professors due to the good pay and comfortable and intellectually engaging work environment. Aspiring professors who do not land jobs at a four-year college should consider job opportunities at community colleges and high schools.

DID YOU KNOW?

US News & World Report recently ranked the career of environmental science and protection technician as one of the top 100 jobs in the United States in terms of a strong job outlook, enjoyable work environment, excellent salary, and other criteria. That's impressive, since there more than 600 different occupations

OPPORTUNITIES IN CANADA

The employment outlook for environmental scientists in Canada varies by specialty and province. For example, job prospects will be good for environmental biologists in the provinces of Alberta, British Columbia, Manitoba, New Brunswick, Nunavut, Prince Edward Island, Quebec, and Saskatchewan, while only fair in Newfoundland and Labrador, Northwest Territories, Nova Scotia, Ontario, and the Yukon Territory. The Canadian government states that "initiatives to address climate change, sustain water resources, and improve research related to the aquatic ecosystem should be a source of work for biologists and scientists." Demand will also increase for biologists to provide advice regarding wildlife management and to create **environmental impact assessments** in provinces where there are a large number of construction projects. Employers of environmental biologists who work with large **data sets** tend to seek job candidates who are proficient in programming languages such as Python, as well as those with strong technical writing skills.

Employment opportunities will be strong for environmental chemists in Prince Edward Island and Quebec, but only fair in Alberta, British Columbia, Manitoba, New Brunswick, Ontario, and Saskatchewan.

Employment outlook information for other environmental science careers in Canada can be found at www.jobbank.gc.ca/trend-analysis/search-job-outlooks.

TECHNOLOGY AND ENVIRONMENTAL SCIENCE

Environmental scientists have come a long way from the days when they recorded their observations and did mathematical computations on paper, relied on sketches and photos as the only source of visually recorded data, and only had the most rudimentary scientific equipment with which to do their work. Today, scientists use cutting-edge technology to collect and analyze data, videoconferencing technology to collaborate with other scientists around the world, and advanced presentation software to convey information to colleagues, managers, and the public. These are just a few of the innovations that have made the work of environmental scientists much easier. The following paragraphs provide more information on some newer types of technology that scientists utilize, and some that are on the horizon.

Environmental scientists are using drones—unmanned aerial vehicles that can be equipped with a variety of equipment such as cameras, Global Positioning Systems (GPS), and sensors (technology that collects information). They use drones to monitor endangered rhinos and other animals, with the end goal of protecting them from poachers; assess the effects of global climate change on birds and other animals; monitor oil spills and their cleanup progress; and survey hard-to-reach bird and other animal habitats.

Scientists are utilizing advanced data analytics tools—combined with **artificial intelligence**—to analyze vast amounts of data in order to better understand scientific information and evaluate efforts to fight environmental problems such as overfishing, global warming, and declining biodiversity.

Scientists and engineers are developing both rigid robots (those that are made of steel and other hard materials) and soft robots (those that are made of soft, elastic materials and that can be used for tasks that rigid robots cannot do) that will clean up oil spills in hard-to-reach areas and remove contaminants from drinking water. These robots will be solar powered so that they will be sustainable and not require additional energy resources.

IN CLOSING

Can you see yourself developing cutting-edge technology that removes pollution from the air, soil, and water? Finding ways to save endangered species? Helping a local government turn a polluted site into a lakeshore park? Conducting research that otherwise protects the environment? Regardless of your interests, a career in environmental science provides many options for those who love the environment and want to use their scientific knowledge and analytical and problem-solving skills to make the world a better place.

Use this book as a starting point to discover even more about careers in environmental science. Get out in the field, and observe environmental scientists as they do their jobs, talk to them about their educational paths and careers, use the resources of professional organizations, and, most importantly, obtain hands-on experience conducting experiments, taking soil and water samples, tracking endangered wildlife, or doing whatever else helps you to explore occupations in environmental science. Good luck on your career exploration!

TEXT-DEPENDENT QUESTIONS:

1. Why is employment demand increasing for environmental scientists?
2. What is the employment outlook for hydrologists?
3. What are soft robots?

RESEARCH PROJECT:

Talk with a conservation scientist, hydrologist, environmental engineer, and other environmental professionals about the future of the field. Ask these and other questions: How will technology change the field? Will educational and training requirements change in the future? What new careers will emerge in the near future? What are some emerging environmental issues that the public may not know about? Write a 500-word report that summarizes your findings, and share it with your science class or environment club.

PHOTO CREDITS

1: Cheryl Kaye, US Fish & Wildlife Service
2–3: US Fish & Wildlife Service
6: Stephen Ausmus, Agricultural Research Service
10: Shannon Bond, Environmental Protection Agency
12: Darren Baker | Shutterstock
13: NASA
17: Susan Middlet, US Fish & Wildlife Service
19: Monica Blaser, US Fish & Wildlife Service
22: US Fish & Wildlife Service
24: Dr. Pablo Clemente-Colon, National Ice Center
25: Gorodenkoff | Shutterstock
28: Macrovector | Shutterstock
30–31: Jerome.Romme | Shutterstock
32: Marten_House | Shutterstock
36: RnDmS | Shutterstock
38: Mark Agnor | Shutterstock
40: Monkey Business Images | Shutterstock

43: Monkey Business Images | Shutterstock
44: Jason Richards, Oak Ridge National Laboratory
47: US Department of Agriculture
50: rkl_foto | Shutterstock
53: Rawpixel.com | Shutterstock
58: Toni Castro, Environmental Protection Agency
61: Gorodenkoff | Shutterstock
62: Gary Peeples, US Fish & Wildlife Service
66: Gary Peeples, US Fish & Wildlife Service
69: drewthehobbit | Shutterstock
70: Sarah Gerrity, US Department of Energy
72: Lisa Hupp, US Fish & Wildlife Service
74: Toni Castro, Environmental Protection Agency
78: AS photostudio | Shutterstock
80: ESB Professional | Shutterstock
83: Deena Green, US Geological Survey
86: Cindy Sandoval, US Fish & Wildlife Service

Cover Photo: Cheryl Kaye, US Fish & Wildlife Service

FURTHER READING

Cunningham, William P. and Mary Ann Cunningham. *Environmental Science: A Global Concern,* 15th ed. New York: McGraw-Hill Education, 2020.

Ignotofsky, Rachel. *The Wondrous Workings of Planet Earth: Understanding Our World and Its Ecosystems.* Berkeley, Calif.: Ten Speed Press, 2018.

Kanoglu, Mehmet, Yunus Cengel, and John Cimbala. *Fundamentals and Applications of Renewable Energy.* New York: McGraw-Hill Education, 2019.

Karr, Susan, Anne Houtman, Jeneen Interlandi. *Environmental Science for a Changing World.* 4th ed. New York: W.H. Freeman & Company, 2021.

Sherman, Daniel J., and David R. Montgomery. *Environmental Science and Sustainability.* New York: W.W. Norton & Company, 2020.

Wallace-Wells, David. *The Uninhabitable Earth: Life After Warming.* New York: Tim Duggan Books, 2020.

INTERNET RESOURCES

www.sciencebuddies.org
This website features a wealth of science experiments for teens, as well as information on more than 160 science careers.

www.bls.gov/ooh/life-physical-and-social-science/environmental-scientists-and-specialists. htm#tab-1
This section of the *Occupational Outlook Handbook* features information on job duties, educational requirements, salaries, and the employment outlook for environmental scientists and specialists.

www.nrel.gov/research/learning.html
This website from the National Renewable Energy Laboratory is a great place to start to learn about the various types of renewable energy—from solar, wind, and bioenergy to geothermal, hydrogen, and advanced vehicles and fuels.

www.niehs.nih.gov/health
This website from the National Institute of Environmental Health Sciences is a great place to start to learn more about environmental topics such as air pollution, climate change, hazardous materials/wastes, hydraulic fracturing and health, pesticides, and water pollution.

www.prospects.ac.uk/job-profiles/browse-sector/environment-and-agriculture
This website provides information on job duties, educational requirements, and career prospects for environmental professionals in the United Kingdom.

www.careers.govt.nz/jobs-database/animal-care-and-conservation/conservation/environmental-scientist
This website from the government of New Zealand provides information on required skills, educational requirements, and job duties for environmental scientists.

INDEX

EDUCATIONAL VIDEO LINKS

Chapter 1:
Learn more about environmental science.
https://www.youtube.com/watch?v=iXge3GLeTXE

Chapter 1:
Learn about the top 10 major global environmental issues in the world.
https://www.youtube.com/watch?v=aTrWtFR_FrQ

Chapter 3:
Professors and students discuss the bachelor of science in environmental sciences program at Northern Arizona University.
https://www.youtube.com/watch?v=a-O6IL6LEgA

Chapter 4:
Learn more about the Maine Envirothon.
https://www.youtube.com/watch?v=D81okyCsFug

AUTHOR BIOGRAPHY

Andrew Morkes has been a writer and editor for more than 25 years. He is the author of more than 50 books and newsletters about college planning and careers, including many titles in the *Cool Careers in Science* series, the *Vault Career Guide to Pharmaceuticals and Biotechnology,* the *College Spotlight* newsletter, and *They Teach That in College!?: A Resource Guide to More Than 100 Interesting College Majors,* which was selected as one of the best books of the year by the library journal *Voice of Youth Advocates.* He is the author and publisher of "The Morkes Report: College and Career Planning Trends" blog and *Nature in Chicagoland: More Than 120 Fantastic Nature Destinations That You Must Visit.* Stories about his work have been published in the *Chicago Tribune, Chicago Sun-Times, Daily Southtown,* and *Practical Homeschooling.* Morkes is also a member of the parent advisory board at his son's school.